RULERS,
SCHOLARS, AND
ARTISTS OF THE
RENAISSANCE™

WILLIAM SHAKESPEARE

England's Greatest Playwright and Poet

RULERS,
SCHOLARS, AND
ARTISTS OF THE
RENAISSANCE™

WILLIAM SHAKESPEARE

England's Greatest Playwright and Poet

David Hilliam

The Rosen Publishing Group, Inc., New York

Published in 2005 by The Rosen Publishing Group, Inc.
29 East 21st Street, New York, NY 10010

Library of Congress Cataloging-in-Publication Data

Hilliam, David.
William Shakespeare: England's greatest playwright and poet/David Hilliam.—1st ed.
    p. cm.-(Rulers, scholars, and artists of the Renaissance)
Includes bibliographical references and index.
ISBN 1-4042-0318-4 (library binding)
1. Shakespeare, William, 1564–1616. 2. Shakespeare, William, 1564–1616—Stage history—To 1625. 3. Dramatists, English—Early modern, 1500–1700—Biography. 4. Theater—England—London—History.
I. Title. II. Series.
PR2895.H55 2005
822.3'3-dc22

                                                          2004009274

Manufactured in the United States of America

On the cover: Background: A circa 1616 engraving of The Globe by Claes Jansz Visscher. Inset: A seventeenth-century portrait believed to be of William Shakespeare, known as the Chandos portrait.

CONTENTS

GREAT BRITAIN AND IRELAND
IN THE TIME OF SHAKESPEARE

SCOTLAND

North Sea

Glasgow ● ● Edinburgh

Atlantic
Ocean

Newcastle ●

ENGLAND

Irish Sea ● York

IRELAND

Dublin ● ● Lincoln

WALES ● Stratford-
upon-Avon

● Cambridge

● Oxford

Bristol ●

● London ● Canterbury

Winchester ● ● Portsmouth

Celtic Sea ● Plymouth

English Channel

FRANCE

INTRODUCTION

Over the last four centuries, William Shakespeare and his plays have developed into a huge and prosperous industry. Shakespeare himself would have been extremely surprised if he had known how frequently his plays—translated into dozens of different languages—would be performed on stages throughout the world. He would be amazed to see the hundreds of thousands of tourists flocking every year to visit his family home in Stratford-upon-Avon. And he would be even more astonished to be told that libraries everywhere would contain not only copies of his plays but also many scholarly studies of every aspect of his work. In nearly every country in the world, university students and schoolchildren read, perform, and

GVLIELMO·SHAKSPEARE
ANNO·POST·MORTEM·CXXIV·
AMOR·PVBLICVS·POSVIT

The Cloud capt Towers
The Gorgeous Palaces
The Solemn Temples,
The Great Globe itself,
Yea all which it Inherit,
Shall Dissolve

WILLIAM SHAKESPEARE 1564 ~ 1616
BURIED AT STRATFORD ~ ON ~ AVON

One hundred and twenty-four years after Shakespeare's death, a memorial statue was erected in London's Westminster Abbey, the royal church of England and site of every coronation since 1066. The carved heads at the base of the statue are believed to be of Queen Elizabeth I, Henry V, and Richard III—his royal patron and two royal subjects of his most important history plays. The figure of Shakespeare leans his elbow on a pile of books, and his left hand points to a scroll that includes a passage from his late play *The Tempest*. The Shakespeare monument is in a part of the abbey called Poet's Corner, which is devoted to Britain's great literary figures.

write essays about his plays. On any given night, dozens of productions of Shakespeare's plays take place in theaters worldwide. Film and television versions of his work—often updated with modern dress and settings—are constantly being produced. No writer in any language has ever become as famous as Shakespeare.

It is impossible to explain in just a few words why Shakespeare deserves this extraordinary reputation. Very often, in this modern age, people who encounter Shakespeare's plays for the first time are puzzled by the strange, old-fashioned words and wonder what all the fuss is about. Shakespeare himself never intended for his plays to be read. He knew exactly what audiences like and how they respond to spectacle, drama, action, and comedy. Therefore, in order to gain a complete appreciation of Shakespeare's artistry, it is essential for students to experience the excitement and thrill of live performances. Merely reading any Shakespeare play is no more satisfying than simply scanning sheet music—for it goes without saying that actors and musicians are needed to bring to vibrant life what is written on the page.

Nevertheless, the quality of Shakespeare's writing—especially in the great tragedies such as *Macbeth, Hamlet, Othello,* or *King Lear*—is so powerful that study of the printed page is necessary to fully enjoy it. During a live performance, so much of what is said can pass quickly by or be poorly heard. It is necessary to refer back to the printed play to really savor and comprehend the rich, poetic language. Few, if any, writers have produced poetry of such compelling beauty as Shakespeare did, not just occasionally, but again and again. Also, no writer has added more words and phrases to the English language than Shakespeare has. Indeed, anyone who speaks English is sure to use some of his phrases on a daily basis even if he or she is unaware of it.

The works of writers, artists, and musicians are often more enjoyable when we know about the lives of those who created them and when we understand the times in which they lived. This account of Elizabethan England and the life and times of William Shakespeare will hopefully increase the pleasure of seeing his work on the stage.

SHAKESPEARE'S BOYHOOD

CHAPTER 1

2

3

4

5

6

William Shakespeare was born in 1564 in Stratford-upon-Avon, in the center of England, just six years after Elizabeth I had become queen. The middle of the sixteenth century was an exciting time to be alive. Political, social, and religious changes were sweeping across Europe, particularly in England. These changes would have a profound effect on the life and work of Shakespeare.

A TIME OF GREAT CHANGE

Three great historical movements were unfolding simultaneously in the mid-sixteenth century. First, it was the age of discovery, when European explorers were eagerly sailing westward to North and South America and eastward to India and the islands of the Pacific.

In 1585, Nicholas Hilliard, a court artist, painted this portrait of Elizabeth I. It is known as the "Ermine Portrait." An ermine, a kind of mink, can be seen perched on Elizabeth's arm, wearing a tiny crown. An ermine was a symbol of royalty, and its fur was often used to trim royal robes.

They were bringing back extraordinary stories of the new and exotic lands and people they had seen.

The sixteenth century was also the age of the Protestant Reformation, when some Catholics began questioning their long-held religious beliefs. These Christians—who came to be known as Protestants for their protests against the Catholic Church and its doctrine—began to think for themselves and deny the authority of the church's head, the pope in Rome.

Finally, it was also the age of the Renaissance, when there was a revival of classical styles of painting and architecture, and the ideas and ideals of the ancient Greeks and Romans were once again circulating throughout western Europe. Added to all this, the invention of printing in the fifteenth century made books widely available for the very first time in human history. This invention was making an extraordinary impact on everyone's lives: new ideas could now be shared in a brief period of time over vast distances.

The effects of all these changes were particularly evident in England. As England was an island with a tradition of seafaring,

This 1519 portrait of Christopher Columbus was painted by Italian artist Sebastiano del Piombo thirteen years after the explorer's death in 1506. Del Piombo, a student of Michelangelo's, was a highly regarded and sought-after artist in his day.

it was inevitable that English ships should quickly follow up on the discoveries made by Christopher Columbus on behalf of Spain. Once it had been discovered that there were vast uncharted territories to be found across the Atlantic Ocean, English sailors were keen to explore them. During Shakespeare's boyhood, many English ships were making voyages to various parts of the Americas. And, when

Shakespeare was sixteen, the exciting news spread throughout England that Francis Drake had just returned to England after sailing around the world, the first Englishman to do so. It was an achievement of which the entire kingdom could be proud.

Happily, the religious conflicts between Catholics and Protestants were beginning to be settled in England. Queen Elizabeth I was anxious to avoid the terrible atrocities committed in the name of religion during the previous reign of her half sister, Queen Mary, who had burned hundreds of Protestants to death. Elizabeth's father, King Henry VIII, had abolished all the Catholic monasteries and shrines of saints throughout Britain. In defiance of Rome, Henry established the Church of England. English people were still God-fearing folk, but they recognized that they were now free from the power of the pope and were no longer expected to believe in all of the Catholic Church's teachings, which at that time could be occasionally harsh, restrictive, and superstitious.

ENGLAND'S NEWFOUND CONFIDENCE

Many of the Catholic monasteries closed by Henry VIII had been turned into stately homes for English noblemen, while others had been turned into grammar schools for clever sons of the middle class. Other

This painting depicts the knighting of the future king Henry V by the then-king Richard II in 1399. Henry was only twelve years old at the time and was helping Richard in his attempts to subdue rebellious Irish lords. Richard's Irish campaign would provide Henry with his first taste of warfare. After gaining the throne in 1413, Henry would spend much of his reign warring with France.

grand homes were being constructed, too, taking inspiration from the Italian Renaissance styles of architecture. England was becoming prosperous as its medieval civil wars were passing into history.

It is little wonder that English people were developing a newfound confidence in themselves and their nation. Nowhere was this better expressed than by William Shakespeare in his series of historical plays. The 1415 Battle of Agincourt, a tremendous victory over the French by the English, is vividly portrayed in his play *Henry V*, and it's impossible not to share the thrill of national pride as young King Henry leads his troops into battle with the words: "God for Harry, England, and Saint George!" (*Henry V* [act 3, scene 1]; Saint George is the patron saint of England.)

Probably the finest expression of this dawning national pride can be found in another of Shakespeare's history plays, *Richard II*, when a nobleman, John of Gaunt, describes the glory of England in his dying speech:

> This royal throne of kings, this
>   sceptre'd isle,
> This earth of majesty, this seat of Mars,
> This other Eden, demi-paradise;
> This fortress, built by Nature for herself
> Against infection and the hand of war;
> This happy breed of men, this little world,
> This precious stone set in the silver sea,
> Which serves it in the office of a wall,
> Or as a moat defensive to a house,
> Against the envy of less happier lands;
> This blessed plot, this earth, this realm,
>   this England . . .
>
> —*Richard II* (act 2, scene 2)

SHAKESPEARE'S CHILDHOOD AND SCHOOL YEARS

It was in this confident country that William Shakespeare was born, probably on April 23, 1564. Appropriately, for a man whose name would come to be synonymous with the glories of England, Shakespeare was born on St. George's Day, the feast day of England's patron saint. The parish register of Holy Trinity Church in Stratford-upon-Avon shows that young William was baptized on April 26, recording his name in Latin as "Gulielmus filius Johannes Shakspere"—William son of John Shakespeare.

It is fortunate that the details of William's birth and family are very well documented for there are periods in his later life about which absolutely nothing is known. William was the eldest son of John and Mary Shakespeare, a prosperous couple who lived in a large house in the center of Stratford-upon-Avon. William grew up there, sharing this home with two younger sisters, Joan and Anne, and three younger brothers, Gilbert, Richard, and Edmund.

Mary Shakespeare, William's mother, was the daughter of a well-to-do local farmer named Robert Arden, who had owned a substantial amount of land and property just outside Stratford and who, upon his death in 1556, had left much of it to Mary.

John Shakespeare, William's father, was a glove-maker and wool-dealer. He must have been a well-liked and well-trusted citizen of the town, for we know that in 1556, he was appointed the "borough taster." This meant that he was in charge of maintaining the standards for all ale and bread produced in Stratford. In 1565, shortly after William was born, John Shakespeare was elected to be an alderman—or senior councillor—of the town. In 1569, when William was five, John Shakespeare became bailiff (mayor) of the borough.

William must have been excited and proud to see his father wearing the official fur-trimmed gown of an alderman as he took charge of much of the town's activities—presiding over the magistrate's court as a justice of the peace, taking the chair at council meetings, going in procession with the other aldermen to church on Sundays, and giving his approval for various events to take place. One such event was the performances put on by traveling players (acting companies) who came to perform in Stratford. When William was five, in 1569, The Queen's Players came to perform in the town's guild-hall. This was probably William's very first experience of theatrical entertainment.

As an alderman of Stratford, John Shakespeare had the privilege of claiming a free place for his son at the local grammar school. When William was about seven years old, he started his studies at the New King's School, near his home on Henley Street. Here, he studied Latin, Greek, ancient history, and rhetoric (the art of speaking persuasively and properly). The discipline at school was strict. In summer, lessons began at six o'clock in the morning and went on until five o'clock, with a two-hour break at midday. In wintertime, the school day was shorter, lasting from seven o'clock in the morning to four in the afternoon. In those darker days, boys were expected to bring their own candles to work by. It's curious to find that boys were punished if they spoke English to one another instead of Latin, the language of formal education. No wonder

A lord mayor and two aldermen of the Elizabethan era are depicted in this illustration. John Shakespeare, William's father, became an alderman of Stratford in 1565. "Alderman" is an Old English term for "elder" or "chief" and denoted a noble of high rank or authority in Anglo-Saxon England. In Elizabethan England, members of local municipal councils were known as aldermen.

The grammar school William Shakespeare attended as a boy in Stratford still stands today *(above right)* at the corner of Church Street and Chapel Lane. Shakespeare probably began attending the grammar school at the age of seven, after completing "petty" school, where he would have been taught the alphabet and how to read. In grammar school, he would have learned Latin and studied the classic Roman authors, whose plays surely inspired Shakespeare's own interest in the dramatic arts.

that in another play, *As You Like It* (act 2, scene 7), Shakespeare writes of

> . . . the whining Schoolboy, with his satchel
> And shining morning face, creeping like
>   a snail
> Unwillingly to school.

QUEEN ELIZABETH I'S VISIT TO KENILWORTH CASTLE

Life for young William Shakespeare was not all hard work and punishment, however. When he was eleven years old, an event took place in the nearby castle at Kenilworth that not only made a deep impression on Shakespeare himself but also changed the entire history of Elizabethan entertainment and literature. No less important a person than Queen Elizabeth herself had traveled from her palace in London to be greeted and honored for three whole weeks by her favorite courtier, Robert Dudley, the great Earl of Leicester. Though Queen Elizabeth never married, it is known that she and Robert Dudley were deeply attached to one another.

No one knows for certain, but it is extremely probable that the Shakespeare family walked over to Kenilworth Castle, about twelve miles (nineteen kilometers) from Stratford, to see some of the extravagant and elaborate entertainments organized by Dudley for the queen. Certainly everyone throughout the entire area would have been talking about the celebrations as their main topic of conversation throughout those summer days in 1575—remembered by historians as the "princely pleasures of Kenilworth." William Shakespeare was no doubt thrilled by Queen Elizabeth's visit and the spectacles put on for her benefit. He could not have known, however, that he, too, would one day offer the queen dazzling entertainment.

THE INVENTION OF THE FIRST MODERN THEATER

When William Shakespeare was a boy, there was no such thing as a permanent public theater devoted exclusively to the presentation of plays anywhere in England. Companies of actors, often called strolling players, traveled from town to town to put on various kinds of dramatic entertainment. These companies were usually patronized by a nobleman and were entitled to wear the livery, or special uniform, of that particular employer. Although they would refer to themselves with grand-sounding titles, such as the Earl of Sussex's Men or Lord Hunsdon's Men, they did not always live at these noblemen's houses but were often based in London, especially in the winter months. In the summer, they would go on tour throughout the country. When they came to a town, if the local authorities agreed, the players would put on their shows in a public building such as the city's guild-hall, the marketplace, or more likely, in the backyard of one of the big inns.

The entertainments they staged would probably be a mixture of clowning, dancing, juggling, acro-batics, and short sketches. At that time, there were very few written plays, but the actors would prob-ably have a repertoire of drama tales based on Bible stories or ancient legends. In an age when there were few diversions from daily toil, the arrival of the strolling players in a town or village was cause for much excitement. Good players were popular and were assured of large and enthusias-tic audiences. The best groups of actors even traveled to Holland, Denmark, and Germany to entertain citizens in foreign cities.

ROBERT DUDLEY'S "PRINCELY PLEASURES"

Robert Dudley, the wealthy Earl of Leicester, lived in a large, imposing castle at Kenilworth and had his own company of players, led by a man called James Burbage. Naturally enough, when Dudley invited Queen Elizabeth to Kenilworth for a lengthy stay, he

Robert Dudley, Earl of Leicester, pictured here in a circa 1575 portrait, first met Elizabeth I when he was eight years old, most likely in the royal classroom in which they were both students. They became good friends, and their friendship lasted throughout their lives. Dudley claimed that he knew her better than anyone else and that she always said that she would never marry. Though at the time it was generally believed that Dudley was born on the same day, in the same year, as Elizabeth, he was probably at least a year older.

was determined to welcome her in a way that she would never forget. She was to stay for three weeks, and the earl decided that throughout her visit, there would be an unending series of all kinds of entertainment. It was a demanding task, for it was known that the queen had sophisticated tastes and would expect only the best. Robert Dudley placed all arrangements for these royal festivities in the hands of James Burbage, an important director of entertainments, and he felt confident that Burbage wouldn't let him down.

Burbage's efforts made the queen's visit a triumphant success. The three-week-long "princely pleasures of Kenilworth" included pageants and dancing on the castle's lawns, music and poetry readings, cannon shooting by day, and fireworks by night. In one spectacular water display on the castle's lake, an actor playing Orion the hunter was seen carrying off the Lady of the Lake on the back of a make-believe dolphin. Queen Elizabeth was delighted. She had brought all her courtiers with her, and everyone enjoyed the hunting, the feasting, and the colorful and surprising spectacles devised by Burbage.

JAMES BURBAGE'S BRILLIANT IDEA

As might be expected, James Burbage became famous as a result of his successful management of the Kenilworth entertainments. When he returned to London in the autumn of 1575, he was wondering how he could build on this success. It was then that he had a brilliant new idea. He would construct a building devoted exclusively to putting on plays and entertainments. In this moment of inspiration, Burbage had invented theaters.

To modern minds, it is surprising that such an idea had never occurred to anyone before. It was inevitable that someone, someday, would realize that a permanent base for the staging of plays would be both popular and profitable—and James Burbage certainly had a good eye for a business opportunity.

In order to make his dream a reality, Burbage borrowed money and rented a piece of land at the far end of a country lane leading northward out of London. This was where he would build his newly invented theater. It was only about a mile and a half (2.5 km) north of the river Thames, but in those days, the built-up area of the city of London was much smaller than it is today, so the field he chose to rent was in open countryside. For example, people used to go to nearby Finsbury Fields to watch or take part in archery practice.

The main reason why James Burbage decided to construct his building outside of the center of London was that the city's mayor and aldermen

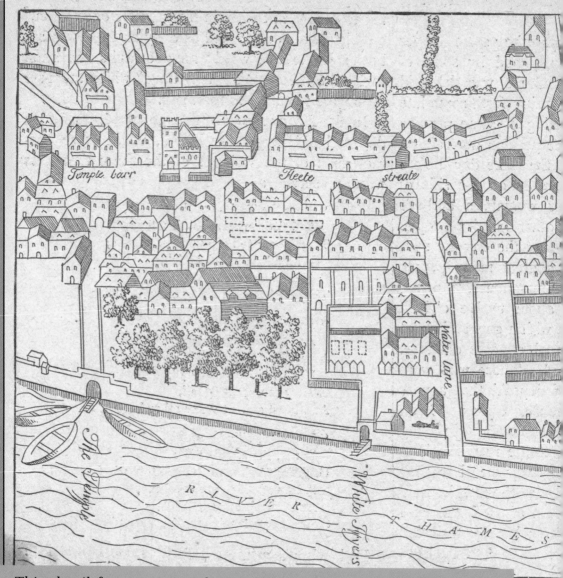

Temple barr   Fleete   streate   Water lane   The Temple   White ffryers   RIVER   THAMES

This detail from a sixteenth-century map of London shows the Fleet Street and Temple Bar areas of the city. At that time, Fleet Street was becoming the city's printing headquarters, specializing in political pamphlets and, by the mid-seventeenth century, newspapers. The Temple Bar is actually a gateway that once marked the limit of the city officials' jurisdiction. Upon this gate, which stands near the law courts, the heads of those executed for treason (plotting against the king or queen) were displayed. During the sixteenth century, London's population almost doubled, thanks mostly to immigration from the countryside. This population boom led city authorities to worry about social unrest, famine, plague, and economic depression.

were not at all in favor of the strolling players. According to them, entertainers caused a nuisance wherever they set up their stages or whenever they drew crowds in inn-yards. In fact, in the city of London, there were many laws and restrictions concerning what players could do and where they could go. By building his theater outside the city, Burbage knew that he would be beyond the control of city authorities.

THE DESIGN OF BURBAGE'S THEATER

Having rented his field on a twenty-one-year lease, James Burbage designed an extraordinary and totally original building—so peculiar and different from any other building that it is difficult to describe. Anyone seeing a picture of it, however, will quickly realize how cleverly Burbage had planned it (see images of the similarly designed Swan and Globe theaters on pages 45 and 48). It was perfectly suited to meet the needs of any group of players wanting to stage their plays.

Burbage's theater was to be circular, three stories high, enclosing a large round area in the middle, where some of the audience could stand. This central area, known as the pit, would be open to the skies. Each of the three circular stories surrounding the pit consisted of a covered gallery containing benches for the rest of the audience. The gallery audiences would be more comfortable than those standing in the pit, not only because they could sit down but also because they were protected from wet weather by having a roof over their heads. Jutting out into the middle of the pit was a large wooden stage for the actors, raised about 5 feet (1.5 meters) from the ground and with a large thatched canopy overhead. Obviously, the audience standing in the pit, who became known as the groundlings, would crowd up close to the actors on the stage and get a good view as they looked up at them.

The main stage was not the theater's only acting area. Above it, on the same level as the middle gallery, was a balcony that could be used by actors in scenes calling for an upstairs room or the top of a castle. Shakespeare would later use this upper part of the stage very effectively for his famous scene in *Romeo and Juliet,* in which Juliet is on the balcony of her house, looking down upon her lover, Romeo. Above this balcony, on the level of the top gallery, was another acting area that could be used not only by actors but also by musicians and the people producing sound effects. At the back of the main stage, there was an inner room that could be used for quieter indoor scenes and that could be curtained off when the action was taking place only on the front of the stage.

As can be seen, James Burbage's strange new building was going to be extremely versatile for the needs of his actors. Having designed it, he wasted no time in getting it constructed. Burbage himself had been a furniture-maker before joining the Earl of Leicester's company of players, and his brother-in-law, John Brayne, was a carpenter. So, with their own expertise and enthusiasm and with the help of others, the huge wooden building soon took shape. Within months it was ready, and in 1576, the year after the "princely pleasures of Kenilworth," Burbage opened its doors to the public. Proudly, he called it The Theatre, which was short for "amphitheater," the name of the large outdoor arenas of entertainment built by the ancient Greeks and Romans, where the earliest tragedies, dramas, and comedies were acted out. Its very name reminded people that it was the first permanent structure built for entertainment since Roman times.

The Theatre was destined, in a few years' time, to play an important part in William Shakespeare's life. At the time of its opening in 1576, however, young William was only twelve years old and still making his daily walk "unwillingly to school."

SHAKESPEARE AND THE LONDON THEATER SCENE

Unfortunately for the Shakespeare family, when William was thirteen years old, some kind of financial disaster hit his father. No one knows exactly what this was, but records indicate that John Shakespeare was getting further and further into debt. The former alderman and high bailiff of Stratford was forced to borrow money by using some of his property as a guarantee for the loan. Legal records show that he was brought to court on a number of occasions for failing to honor his debts. He seems to have lived in fear of being beaten up by creditors.

At one time, according to Stratford's town records, he even asked for legal protection against four particularly unpleasant individuals who apparently threatened "death and mutilation of his limbs."

William Shakespeare's father, John, was a middle-class glove-maker who was sufficiently well-regarded to be nominated to positions of local power, rising from constable and chamberlain of Stratford to bailiff and eventually chief alderman. Yet he did manage to get into trouble with the law more than once. He was accused twice of illegal wool dealing, he was sued by creditors, and he appeared on a list of "papists" (Catholics) who failed to take Protestant communion. This document includes a reference to John Shakespeare *(circled)*, accusing him of illegally lending money at interest.

His father's troubles almost certainly resulted in William having to leave school at the age of about fourteen or fifteen, without any prospect of going to a university. Exactly what he did after he left school is a mystery. People have suggested that he may have been a schoolmaster for a while, but there is no evidence to back up this theory. Perhaps he simply remained in his father's workshop, helping to skin animals to make leather. Perhaps he sold gloves in the town market. No one knows.

However, what is certain is that when he was eighteen, he fell in love with a young woman

Anne Hathaway's Cottage, pictured above, was the home of William Shakespeare's wife before they married in 1582. It is located in Shottery, a small hamlet about one mile (1.5 km) from Stratford's town center. Descendants of the Hathaways continued to occupy the home until 1892, when the Shakespeare Birthplace Trust purchased the property.

named Anne Hathaway. Eight years older than Shakespeare, she was the daughter of one of his father's friends, a prosperous farmer who lived in the nearby village of Shottery, just 1 mile (1.5 km) from the center of Stratford. Today, tourists can still look around the substantial timber-framed and thatched building formerly owned by the Hathaway family and known today as Anne Hathaway's Cottage.

William had to receive special permission to marry, since he was still legally a minor. However,

both families were agreeable, so Anne and William
were married on November 30, 1582. They began
their married life by moving in with William's parents
in their home on Henley Street (Shakespeare's birthplace). Anne and William's baby girl was born there
just six months later and was baptized with the name
Susanna. Then, in 1585, twins were born to them: a
girl, Judith, and a boy, Hamnet.

SHAKESPEARE MOVES TO LONDON

It might be supposed that providing for a wife and
three young children would have kept the twenty-one-
year-old William Shakespeare closely linked to
Stratford. Surprisingly, however, for the next few
years, there is no historical record detailing where he
was or what he was doing. Sometimes these are called
Shakespeare's "lost years," and it is likely that this
period of his life will always remain a mystery. At
first, he remained with his young family, but by the
year 1588, it seems clear that he had gone to London,
often finding some kind of employment with a company of actors. By 1592, he was beginning to write his
earliest plays.

It has to be admitted that very little is known
of the details of Shakespeare's adult life. From

1592 on, he is known almost entirely through his writings and by various comments people made about him at the time. His first two plays were probably the comedies *The Two Gentlemen of Verona* and *The Taming of the Shrew*, both set in Italy. So many of his plays have an Italian background that there is a strong possibility that some of his lost years were actually spent in Italy.

The London in which he settled in the late 1580s was filled with exciting possibilities for an ambitious actor and playwright. By then, James Burbage's Theatre was more than ten years old. It had been a tremendous success from the very start. Burbage made so much money with it that the year following its opening, 1577, he built a second playhouse right next to it, called The Curtain. It was so called because it was built on a plot of land named Curtain Field. Even today, there is a street in this area called Curtain Road. It was in The Theatre and The Curtain that Shakespeare's earliest plays were staged.

As Shakespeare wrote more and more, his life and fortune became closely linked with James Burbage and his son, Richard Burbage, who was a brilliant actor, roughly the same age as Shakespeare himself. The acting company that played for Burbage was called The Chamberlain's Men. Shakespeare belonged to The Chamberlain's Men and soon established himself as the company's key figure as he acted and wrote his plays for it. He was lucky to become attached to this company of actors early in his London days, and the company in turn was lucky to have Shakespeare writing for it. This strong partnership lasted all of Shakespeare's professional life and enabled him to write play after play without worrying about where he could have them performed. No one else in London at that time enjoyed the same professional stability as Shakespeare did for over twenty years.

SHAKESPEARE'S FAMILY IN STRATFORD

While William Shakespeare was enjoying a busy and successful life working in London, his parents; his wife, Anne; and his three children remained at home in Stratford-upon-Avon. William must have traveled the road between London and Stratford many times, commuting between his workplace and his family home. Unfortunately for historians, he kept his private life quite separate from his public life, and we can only

NON SANZ DROICT

The Armorial Bearings of
WILLIAM SHAKESPEARE
of Stratford-upon-Avon.

J. D. Heaton-Armstrong

College of Arms,
London.

Chester Herald
and Registrar.

This is a rendering of the Shakespeare family's coat of arms. John Shakespeare, William's father, tried more than once to obtain a coat of arms. His first attempt was unsuccessful. Near the end of John Shakespeare's life, however, he once again applied to the College of Heralds, and, probably due to William's growing fame, this time his wish was granted. On October 20, 1596, by permission of the Garter King of Arms, John Shakespeare and his descendants were permitted to display on their door and personal items a gold coat of arms, with a black banner bearing a silver spear (a visual representation of the family name Shakespeare). The motto was "Non sanz droict," or "Not without right."

guess at the details. What is certain is that William maintained close ties with both his parents and his wife, supporting them financially as his writing earned him more and more wealth and fame in London.

Sadly, his only son, Hamnet—one of the twins— died in 1596, at the age of eleven and was buried in Stratford. We don't even know if Shakespeare was able to attend the funeral. It must have been a difficult time for his family, especially for Anne, who was left alone so much of the time to bring up their children. William and Anne were now left with just the two girls, Susanna, thirteen years old, and Judith, the remaining twin, eleven years old.

A happier fact concerns John Shakespeare, William's father. It seems that he managed to recover his good name and his fortune, probably thanks to William's help. Two months after young Hamnet's death, John was granted a coat of arms (a heraldic shield), giving him and his descendants—including William—the status of gentlemen.

Another happy fact to note is that in the following year, 1597, William Shakespeare had become so wealthy that he bought a large house, called New Place, for himself and his family right in the middle of Stratford. This was the second- biggest house in town and was to be his home for the rest of his life. He retired there in 1611, and this was where he died in 1616.

RIVAL PLAYWRIGHTS

Naturally enough, the very existence of Burbage's two theaters in London acted as a magnet to attract new and talented playwrights who hoped to see their work produced on the stage. The most famous playwright at that time was a young man named Christopher Marlowe, who was exactly the same age as Shakespeare himself. Marlowe had just left Cambridge University and was becoming notorious for his wild lifestyle and antireligious views. He was also engaged as a government spy for Queen Elizabeth. Marlowe's skill at writing plays was quite exceptional, and his first play, *Tamburlaine*, produced in 1587, took London by storm. Among his other plays, *Dr. Faustus* is probably the best-known and most intriguing, being the story of a man who sells his soul to the devil in return for learning all kinds of secret knowledge.

Though a brilliant playwright, Marlowe seemed to court danger. In 1593, at the age of twenty-nine, he was stabbed to death in a London pub. Marlowe's death came at the beginning of

The Tragicall History
of the Life and Death
of *Doctor Faustus.*

Written by *Ch. Mar*

LONDON,
Printed for *Iohn Wright*, and are to be sold at his shop
Without Newgate, at the ʃ... ...he
Bi⸍ 1636⸍

Like Shakespeare, Christopher Marlowe came from middle-class origins. His father was a shoemaker and his mother was a farmer's daughter. Like Shakespeare's father, Marlowe's father often found himself in trouble with the law, usually for nonpayment of debts. Marlowe is generally thought of as the greatest English dramatist before Shakespeare. They were born in the same year, but Marlowe died at the age of twenty-nine after a barroom stabbing. His 1588 play, *Dr. Faustus*, is considered his greatest work. The title page to a 1616 edition of the play appears above.

Shakespeare's own writing career, and Shakespeare was suddenly left with no serious rivals. As a result, he became London's foremost playwright. Plays by other writers at this time, such as John Lyly, Robert Greene, or George Peele, have survived, but anyone who reads them today will instantly recognize that Shakespeare's genius towers above them all.

MORE THEATERS ARE BUILT

Given the popularity of both The Theatre and The Curtain, it wasn't long before other theaters began to spring up. Burbage's main rival in theater building was a wealthy and energetic businessman named Philip Henslowe. In 1587, just before Shakespeare arrived in London, Henslowe built a playhouse closely resembling The Theatre on the south bank of the river Thames in the area called Bankside. Like Burbage, Henslowe had chosen to build his theater well away from the center of the city of London, so as to avoid the restrictions of the city authorities. This new theater was called The Rose, and over the following years, Philip Henslowe spent his profits on enlarging and improving it. The company of actors that played there was called The Admiral's Men. By far the most successful of their actors was Edward Alleyn, who made so much money that, with great generosity, he founded a famous school, Dulwich College, which is still one of the foremost schools in England.

Bankside was traditionally a place for entertainment because there were fewer houses on this south bank of the Thames. It was an area where Londoners had long enjoyed bull-baiting, bear-baiting, and cock-fighting. It is little wonder that in 1595 another theater was built there, which was called The Swan. Built by a man called Francis Langley, The Swan posed a threat to both Burbage and Henslowe. Henslowe's response to Langley's new theater was to build yet another playhouse on the north side of the river Thames, which he called The Fortune. Although this was within the city limits, at least he had no other competing theater immediately nearby.

At this time in the late 1590s, the future of James Burbage's original playhouse, The Theatre, was in doubt, not because it was unpopular but because the lease on the land was due to expire. James Burbage had taken this lease in 1576 for twenty-one years, so in 1597, it was due for renewal.

The problem was that when James Burbage wrote to the landlord who owned the land, asking to renew the lease, he received no reply. The fact is, the landlord knew how profitable The Theatre had become and he planned to refuse to let Burbage continue on his land so that he could own The Theatre for himself. Burbage became so frustrated over the situation, wondering what to do next, that he neglected his health, fell ill, and died.

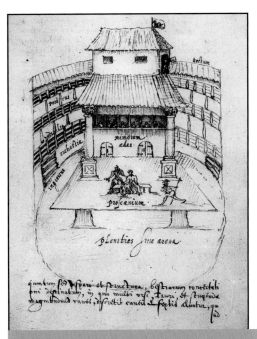

The interior of The Swan is seen in this circa 1596 sketch by Johannes de Witt. De Witt sketched the theater after attending a play there. His friend Arend van Buchell made this copy of de Witt's original sketch. The Swan was built circa 1595 by Francis Langley in Bankside, London.

"VERY RIOTOUS, OUTRAGEOUS AND FORCIBLE"

The death of James Burbage, and the legal difficulty of owning a theater on someone else's land, presented a real problem to Burbage's two sons, Richard and Cuthbert, who had inherited The Theatre. The trouble increased when the landlord tried to prevent them from entering the building, complaining that they were trespassing on his land. Drastic action was needed, so Richard and Cuthbert made the bold decision to pull The Theatre down and rebuild it elsewhere. And what better place than on Bankside, which was rapidly developing into London's premier entertainment center!

The immediate difficulty for Richard and Cuthbert was that they did not have enough money to undertake this expensive and labor-intensive move. Therefore, they decided to invite the most important members of The Chamberlain's Men—Burbage's company—to get together and form a syndicate. Each member of the syndicate would put money into the venture and then share the profits. The two Burbage brothers were joined by five others: William Shakespeare, John Heminges, William Kemp, Augustine Phillips, and Thomas Pope. By this time, Shakespeare was already becoming well-paid and famous for his playwriting, but this new investment was going to make his fortune.

Just after Christmas in 1598, the Burbage brothers, Shakespeare, and the other members of the syndicate hired a master carpenter, Peter Street, to undertake the complicated task of dismantling The Theatre, transporting it to Bankside, and rebuilding it on the new site they had rented. However, as soon as Peter Street began this demolition work, the landlord sent a party of men to prevent him. Arguments and fighting soon broke out, resulting in the landlord taking the Burbage brothers to court and suing them for trespassing and theft.

Court records provide an interesting picture of what happened. According to the landlord's account, the Burbage party

> . . . then and there armed themselves with diverse and many unlawful and offensive weapons, as namely swords, daggers, bills [battle-axes], axes and such like, and so armed did then repair [go] unto the said Theatre, and then and there armed as aforesaid, in very riotous, outrageous and forcible manner . . . attempted to pull down the said Theatre . . . pulling, breaking and throwing down the said Theatre in very outrageous, violent and riotous sort.

THE GLOBE

This engraving of The Globe was made by the Amsterdam artist Claes Jansz Visscher in 1616, the year of Shakespeare's death.

The task of transporting all the heavy timbers of The Theatre along London's narrow roads and across London Bridge must have taken many trips of Peter Street's horse-drawn carts. Despite the landlord's protests, however, and the complexity of the move, the work went ahead incredibly quickly. Early in 1599, the new playhouse was ready to open. The chaotic manner in which the materials were brought to Bankside must have been a major topic of conversation throughout London, providing good publicity for Richard Burbage, Shakespeare, and The Chamberlain's Men.

Boldly, the site of the new playhouse was only about 50 yards (45 meters) from its rival theater, The Rose, where Philip Henslowe and his Admiral's

Men were putting on their plays. Clearly the choice of this site was an act of defiance. From now on, the two playhouses competed even more fiercely for their audiences.

So it was here, in Burbage's new theater, that Shakespeare's later and greatest plays appeared on stage for the first time. A fresh name had to be found for this new playhouse. The company must have discussed it among themselves before a final decision was made. No one knows who proposed the name that was ultimately chosen. More than likely, it was Shakespeare himself who thought it up. At any rate, his name is linked with it forever.

It was to be called The Globe.

SHAKESPEARE'S PLAYS AND POEMS

CHAPTER 4

William Shakespeare was not only a brilliant playwright and poet, but he was also extremely productive. The timeline of Shakespeare's works on pages 56 and 57 proves just how actively creative Shakespeare was. His output averaged about two plays a year over a period of twenty years!

Shakespeare's plays fall roughly into four categories: comedies, histories, tragedies, and a small group at the end of his writing career that are difficult to define. These final plays are neither tragedies nor comedies but contain elements of both and all end happily. Up to the opening of The Globe in 1599, Shakespeare mostly wrote comedies and histories. From 1599 onward, he wrote a succession of remarkable and powerful tragedies and then ended his rich career of plays with the beautiful and strange final group of plays.

When Shakespeare arrived in London in the early 1590s, he began his writing career with the comedies *The Two Gentlemen of Verona* and *The Taming of the Shrew*. He also began a series of dramas based on English history with a play about the reign of King Henry VI, who was murdered in a civil war known as the War of the Roses. However, in 1593, just as Shakespeare was beginning to make a name for himself in London, the plague struck the city. Outbreaks of the plague (a terrible disease that killed its victims within days) were common in London, especially in the summer months. In an attempt to prevent the plague from spreading, the city authorities ordered all London theaters to be closed. The result was that actors and playwrights were temporarily out of work. Luckily, at this time Shakespeare was helped financially by a young nobleman, the Earl of Southampton. As thanks for this patronage, Shakespeare wrote his long poems *Venus and Adonis* and *The Rape of Lucrece*, dedicating them to the young earl.

In 1594, the theaters opened again. This was the start of Shakespeare's nonstop production of plays, which lasted until he retired and returned to Stratford in 1611.

he weekly Burials of the City of LONDON, and the Parishes adjacent to the

y pity on this sinfull Land,   Have   We so wicked been, that thou canst not

This seventeenth-century engraving shows the weekly burials that occurred outside London during an outbreak of the plague, or black death. A skeleton holding an hourglass and a spear—symbols of mortality and death—presides over the burials. The plague struck London several times early in the century and in 1665 killed more than 100,000 people.

SHAKESPEARE'S STYLE

Anyone reading Shakespeare for the first time may be slightly puzzled to see the form in which his plays are written. Much of his work consists of lines of verse with ten syllables to a line, sometimes in what are called rhyming couplets. This means that the lines of the play proceed in pairs whose endings rhyme. For example, in his comedy *A Midsummer Night's Dream* (act 2, scene 1), Oberon, the king of the fairies, is given these lines:

> I know a bank where the wild thyme blows,
> Where oxslips and the nodding violet grows;
> Quite over-canopied with luscious
>   woodbine,
> With sweet musk-roses, and with eglantine:
> There sleeps Titania sometime of the night,
> Lulled in these flowers with dances
>   and delight;
> And there the snake throws her
>   enamelled skin,
> Weed wide enough to wrap a fairy in . . .

Shakespeare's earlier plays often contain rhyming couplets like these, but Shakespeare was never bound by rules and always wrote as he felt the occasion demanded.

Increasingly, he wrote in what is called blank verse, which also contains lines with ten syllables but no rhyming endings. This, of course, is much more freely flowing language, closer to the rhythms of everyday speech. Most of his later plays were written in blank verse. However, he always felt free to add rhymes if he felt like it and often ended a scene with a powerful rhyming couplet to signify that an incident had come to an end. A good example is from *Macbeth*, in the scene in which Macbeth decides to kill Banquo. The scene ends with these words:

> It is concluded: Banquo thy soul's flight,
> If it find heaven, must find it out to-night.
> —*Macbeth*, (act 3, scene 1)

For comic scenes in which servants and low-born people are depicted, Shakespeare used ordinary prose, and when kings or lords enter, he changed back to write in blank verse, which sounds more elevated and formal. Such differences in language are subconsciously felt by the audience, and actors know how to express this change of mood. It is worth noting that blank verse is a great help to actors who are learning their lines. In fact, it's much easier to learn than ordinary prose. The firm rhythms and regular line lengths are easier to commit to memory. In this, Shakespeare, as a good craftsman, was helping his company of players.

This painting depicts a scene from one of Shakespeare's most popular plays, the tragedy *Macbeth* (1606), showing Macbeth *(left)*, Banquo *(right)*, and the Three Witches *(far right)*. Early in the play, Macbeth and Banquo meet these witches, usually referred to as the Weird Sisters, and receive their prophecy that Macbeth shall become king.

THE SONNETS

A sonnet is a short fourteen-line poem with strict rules about structure and rhyme scheme. This kind of poem has been popular with many writers, but Shakespeare seems to have been particularly fond of the sonnet form. He wrote a series of no fewer than 154 sonnets during the 1590s, in which he seemed to express his personal thoughts and emotions, often about love relationships. Some of Shakespeare's

A TIMELINE OF SHAKESPEARE'S WORKS

1590–1591	Comedy	*The Two Gentlemen of Verona*
1590–1591	Comedy	*The Taming of the Shrew*
1591	History	*Henry VI (Part Two)*
1591	History	*Henry VI (Part Three)*
1592	History	*Henry VI (Part One)*
1592–1593	Tragedy	*Titus Andronicus*
1592–1593	History	*Richard III*
1592–1593	Poem	*Venus and Adonis*
1593–1594	Poem	*The Rape of Lucrece*
1594	Poems	From this date Shakespeare began writing his 154 sonnets. These were collected and published in 1609.
1594	Comedy	*The Comedy of Errors*
1594–1595	Comedy	*Love's Labour's Lost*
1595	History	*Richard II*
1595	Tragedy	*Romeo and Juliet*
1595	Comedy	*A Midsummer Night's Dream*
1596	History	*King John*
1596–1597	Comedy	*The Merchant of Venice*
1596–1597	History	*Henry IV (Part One)*
1597–1598	Comedy	*The Merry Wives of Windsor*
1597–1598	History	*Henry IV (Part Two)*
1598	Comedy	*Much Ado About Nothing*
1598–1599	History	*Henry V*
1599	Tragedy	*Julius Caesar*
1599–1600	Comedy	*As You Like It*
1600–1601	Tragedy	*Hamlet*

1601	Comedy	*Twelfth Night*
1602	Tragedy	*Troilus and Cressida*
1603	Comedy*	*Measure for Measure*
1603–1604	History	*Sir Thomas More*
1603–1604	Tragedy	*Othello*
1604–1605	Comedy	*All's Well That Ends Well*
1605	Tragedy	*Timon of Athens*
1605–1606	Tragedy	*King Lear*
1606	Tragedy	*Macbeth*
1606	Tragedy	*Antony and Cleopatra*
1607	Comedy*	*Pericles*
1608	Tragedy	*Coriolanus*
1609	Comedy*	*The Winter's Tale*
1610	Comedy*	*Cymbeline*
1611	Comedy*	*The Tempest*
1613	History	*Henry VIII* (written in collaboration with others)

* *Some of the later plays are difficult to put into any category, as they contain many different elements. However, as they have happy endings, they are listed here as comedies.*

The dates of some plays are still uncertain, but the dates given here are those given in *The Oxford Companion to Shakespeare*, edited by Michael Dobson and Stanley Wells, published in 2001 by Oxford University Press.

sonnets are addressed to a young nobleman, and some of the others are written to a young woman— a "dark lady"—but despite a great deal of research and numerous guesses, no one knows who these people were.

THE COMEDIES

In the first ten years of his writing career, from 1591 to 1601, Shakespeare wrote ten comedies. Some are more popular and more frequently produced than others. Three of them, in particular, are often considered as being among the best, although this will always be a matter of personal choice. They are *A Midsummer Night's Dream* (1595), *The Merchant of Venice* (1596–1597), and *Twelfth Night* (1601). Then, after 1601, Shakespeare turned away from comedies and began to concentrate instead on writing tragedies.

There were no actresses in Shakespeare's time because, in Elizabethan times, it was thought to be indecent for women to take part in acting on the stage. Therefore, all female roles were taken by boys. Of course, this gave an opportunity for plots with amusing and confusing situations in which female characters, in order to disguise themselves for one reason or another, pretended they were

This ledger page is from the accounts of Edmund Tylney, master of the revels from 1579 to 1610. The master of the revels supervised all royal festivities. Under Tylney, the office began to censor the content of plays if it was seen to criticize the king or queen or incite people to riot. This page includes Tylney's references to four of Shakespeare's plays—*The Merry Wives of Windsor, Measure for Measure, The Comedy of Errors*, and *Love's Labour's Lost*. Tylney appears to mistakenly refer to the playwright as "Shaxberd."

young men. So young men were acting the parts of young women acting as young men! In *The Merchant of Venice*, for example, the heroine, called Portia, disguises herself as a young male lawyer. Her maid, Nerissa, pretends to be her male secretary. In this role of lawyer, Portia successfully defends her lover in a difficult lawsuit. The changing of sexes is a frequent dramatic trick in Shakespeare's comedies. Partly because the acting profession was a male-only domain, there are relatively few female parts in any of Shakespeare's plays, especially the histories, which are devoted to the exploits of male leaders and soldiers.

THE HISTORIES

Shakespeare almost always took the plots of his plays from other people's books, and one book in particular provided him with material for many of his plays. This was *The Chronicles of England, Scotland and Ireland*, published in 1577 by English writer Raphael Holinshed. This history of England was so popular that it was reprinted in an enlarged edition in 1587, just about the same time that Shakespeare arrived in London to begin his career. Holinshed's *Chronicles* was the most complete

Mr. WILLIAM

SHAKESPEARES

COMEDIES,
HISTORIES, &
TRAGEDIES.

Published according to the True Originall Copies.

Martin Droeshout sculpsit London.

LONDON
Printed by Isaac Iaggard, and Ed. Blount. 1623.

This portrait of William Shakespeare appears on the title page of the First Folio of his works, published in 1623, seven years after his death. The First Folio was the first collected edition of Shakespeare's plays. It included thirty-six plays, eighteen of which had never been published before. The editors of the volume were Shakespeare's fellow actors John Heminges and Henry Condell. They were the first to arrange his plays in three genres—comedies, histories, and tragedies—a system of classification that is still used today.

history of the British Isles written up to that point. It inspired Shakespeare not only to write about the medieval English kings but also about the Scottish king Macbeth and the semi-legendary Celtic figures of Cymbeline and King Lear.

Although Shakespeare did not write his history plays in chronological order, he did in fact cover about a hundred years of English history, from the late fourteenth to the late fifteenth century. In them, he describes the events of the successive reigns of King Richard II (1377–1399), Henry IV (1399–1413), Henry V (1413–1422), Henry VI (1422–1471), Edward IV (1471–1483), and Richard III (1483–1485). He also wrote a play about the earlier reign of King John (1199–1216). At the end of his life, he collaborated with the playwright John Fletcher to write about the reign of Queen Elizabeth I's father, King Henry VIII (1509–1547). As can be seen, this broad dramatic sweep provides a very generous overview of more than 300 years of historical events and characters. Indeed, many English people have learned much of their nation's history through reading and seeing these plays.

Richard II was deposed (forced to step down from the throne) by his successor, who became Henry IV. Therefore Shakespeare's play *Richard II*, concerning a successful rebellion, was regarded as too dangerous to put on the stage toward the end of Queen Elizabeth's reign, when it was known that some of her enemies were plotting against her. It was feared that such a play might encourage an all-out rebellion against the queen herself. On the other hand, Richard III, who had been killed in battle by Queen's Elizabeth's grandfather, Henry VII, was portrayed as a hunchbacked monster by Shakespeare. His distorted, grotesque character is seen by many as propaganda for Queen Elizabeth's Tudor family and against her grandfather's enemy, Richard. Shakespeare's history plays, therefore, were seen as having political relevance to his own times, even when the action they depicted occurred more than a hundred years earlier.

Perhaps the most exciting of Shakespeare's history plays is *Henry V*, which describes a triumphant and decisive English victory over the French at the Battle of Agincourt (1415), which became known as one of the greatest moments of English history. Naturally, Shakespeare's audiences liked to be reminded of such a victory, especially after Sir Francis Drake had just inflicted a similar overwhelming defeat over the Spanish Armada in 1588.

THE TRAGEDIES

There's no doubt that Shakespeare's greatest works
are his tragedies. No other writer in the English language has ever produced such powerful drama as
these. It is impossible to describe them properly in
just a few paragraphs, for they need to be seen and
experienced on the stage and also studied in depth.
The general consensus is that Shakespeare's best
tragedies include *Macbeth, Hamlet, Julius Caesar,
Othello, Antony and Cleopatra*, and *King Lear*. For anyone who is new to Shakespeare, probably the most
easily understood tragedy is *Macbeth*, which is
short and very action-packed.

Queen Elizabeth I died in 1603 and was suc-
ceeded by King James of Scotland, who was
passionately interested in the supernatural. He had
even written a book about witchcraft. Shakespeare
wrote *Macbeth* specially to please the king, for it is
set in eleventh-century Scotland and concerns the
evil power of three witches who tempt a Scottish
nobleman (Macbeth) to murderous ambition by
telling him he will be king. It is a play filled with
witches, ghosts, sword fights, and strange happen-
ings. There are even ghostly apparitions of a long
line of Scottish kings, all of whom, of course, were
King James's own ancestors.

STROLERS PERFORMING HAMLET BEFORE THE SQUIRE.

Strolling players are seen performing a scene from *Hamlet* for a rather uninterested squire and his wife in this eighteenth-century engraving. From medieval times to the present day, groups of strolling players have toured England performing plays. In Shakespeare's time, these plays were performed in barns and in the courtyards of inns. The English government did not approve of strolling players, who they felt spread rebellion and disease. In 1572, a law was passed banning strolling players from touring the country. The only actors allowed to perform were those employed by noblemen. These noblemen formed acting companies of the sort Shakespeare joined, and eventually they built their own permanent theaters.

Hamlet is about a young prince who one night encounters the ghost of his recently deceased father. He learns that his father was murdered by his mother and new stepfather. From that moment on, Hamlet is desperate to avenge his father, but he is paralyzed by indecisiveness about how to do it. He is even driven to consider suicide ("To be, or not to be: that is the question") when his confusion is at its greatest. He eventually does avenge his father, but Hamlet is then killed by a poisoned weapon in a sword fight.

Unlike *Hamlet*, *Julius Caesar* is a tragedy based on real history—the assassination of the Roman dictator Julius Caesar. This play, too, features supernatural events, including a fortune-teller and ghostly dreams. *Othello* is a story about jealousy, in which a husband wrongly suspects his wife of being unfaithful to him and strangles her in her bedroom. *Antony and Cleopatra* portrays the love between a Roman general, Mark Antony, who was a relation of Julius Caesar's, and the exotically beautiful Cleopatra, queen of Egypt. The two lovers join together in war but are defeated by Augustus Caesar at the naval battle of Actium. Antony kills himself by falling on his sword, and Cleopatra, desperate at hearing of his death, commits suicide by holding poisonous snakes to her breast.

King Lear is perhaps the most emotionally turbulent drama Shakespeare wrote. It is about an aging and increasingly senile king, Lear, who makes terrible misjudgments about his daughters. The two older daughters, Goneril and Regan, are cruel, greedy, and ambitious, while Lear's youngest, Cordelia, is loyal and loving. Easily deceived by their empty flattery, Lear favors Goneril and Regan and disinherits the obedient and affectionate Cordelia. It is a play about ingratitude, rejection, and lack of true understanding. King Lear goes mad, and when he becomes sane again, he realizes his mistakes. However, it is too late. Enemies have killed his true daughter, Cordelia, and he enters the stage carrying her corpse in his arms. In his anguished grief, he goes mad again and dies. Meanwhile, Goneril has poisoned her sister Regan and has stabbed herself to death.

THE FINAL GROUP OF PLAYS

The emotions in Shakespeare's tragedies are so intense that some critics believe that Shakespeare himself was suffering from a nervous breakdown at the time of their writing and that the plays reflect his own mental turmoil. But as with almost everything about Shakespeare's private life, no one can definitively prove this.

However, after 1607, Shakespeare's plays become more calm and tranquil, as if the playwright had passed through a difficult period of his

SHAKESPEARE'S LANGUAGE

Above all, Shakespeare's genius is found in the extraordinary range of his vocabulary. He had an unequaled gift for finding just the right words. In fact, he often invented the right words to suit a given situation. These new terms have remained in the English language ever since. *Accommodation, assassination, dexterously, dislocate, indistinguishable, obscene, premeditate, reliance,* and *submerged* are just a few of almost 2,000 words Shakespeare added to the language.

Also, Shakespeare's gift for finding unforgettable phrases has introduced countless sayings into the language. Some of the most often-used include *more in sorrow than in anger, into thin air, green-eyed jealousy, a virtue of necessity, tongue-tied, a tower of strength, too much of a good thing, a fool's paradise, without rhyme or reason, knitted your brows, bloody-minded,* and *more sinned against than sinning.* The list could go on and on. Readers and listeners will find echoes of phrases they have known and used all their lives without, perhaps, realizing that they have been quoting William Shakespeare all along.

life and had now achieved serenity and the calm wisdom and insight of experience. The last group of plays adopts a very different tone compared with those of Shakespeare's earlier periods and creates a very different ambience. They are *Pericles, Cymbeline, The Winter's Tale,* and *The Tempest.* Of these, the last two are the most popular and frequently performed.

Interestingly, a young woman features prominently in each of these final plays, and Shakespeare gives them unusual and strangely meaningful names. In *Pericles,* there is Marina—literally "coming from the sea." In *The Winter's Tale,* there is Perdita—literally "the lost one" (who is ultimately found). Finally, in *The Tempest,* there is Miranda—literally "the girl of wonder." These young women remind us of Lear's daughter Cordelia, and it almost seems as if Shakespeare is still haunted by her death. No final conclusion can be drawn from these allegorical names, but readers may recognize that these young women seem to provide a psychological thread that draws Shakespeare's final plays together.

The Tempest was Shakespeare's last solo-authored play. It is set on an island where Prospero and his daughter, Miranda, live together with a misshapen, half-human monster named Caliban (the son of a

The corporate headquarters of the British Broadcasting Corporation (BBC) in London features this sculpture by Eric Gill of Prospero and Ariel, two characters from Shakespeare's late play *The Tempest*. The wizard Prospero is depicted sending the fairylike Ariel out into the world. Three other Gill sculptures of Ariel decorate the building's facade. Ariel, as an invisible spirit of the air, was seen as a poetic symbol of broadcasting.

witch) and a lively, fairy-like creature named Ariel. Twelve years prior, Prospero had been the Duke of Milan, but his brother Antonio had ousted him from his throne and turned him adrift in a boat with his infant daughter. As Prospero had knowledge of magic, he was able to control Caliban and Ariel, the original inhab-itants of the island on which the exiles landed. They then became Pros-pero's servants. It is a strange island, on which supernatural forces are at work.

The play begins with a storm at sea, as a result of which Antonio, Prospero's scheming brother, is shipwrecked with his companions on the same island where Prospero and Miranda have been living for twelve years. It is no ordinary storm and shipwreck, however, for both are brought about by the magical force of Prospero, who resembles a wise and kindly wizard. *The Tempest* includes all the ingredients of tragedy, but Prospero manages to control all of these elements and characters and bring about a happy ending for everyone, except, perhaps, for Caliban. It is not difficult to see Shakespeare himself as the character of Prospero. In one of the wizard's final speeches (act 4, scene 1), it seems as if the playwright is bidding farewell to his audience as he prepares to retire to Stratford:

Our revels now are ended. These our actors,
As I foretold you, were all spirits, and
Are melted into air, into thin air;
And, like the baseless fabric of this vision,
The cloud-capp'd towers, the
    gorgeous palaces,
The solemn temples, the great globe itself,
Yea, all which it inherits, shall dissolve,
And like this insubstantial pageant faded,
Leave not a rack behind. We are such stuff
As dreams are made on; and our little life
Is rounded with a sleep . . .

Did Shakespeare think of his famous theater, The Globe, when he wrote these lines? It's certainly

tempting to think so. In any case, this speech is a
memorable and appropriate conclusion to the
twenty years of Shakespeare's astonishingly creative professional life.

SHAKESPEARE'S FINAL YEARS

1
2
3
4
6

CHAPTER 5

When Queen Elizabeth I died in 1603, Shakespeare was at the height of his writing career and was just beginning to produce his great series of tragedies. He had gained both wealth and reputation. He was enjoying a busy life, acting and producing plays for his friend Richard Burbage, with whom he had now worked for well over ten years. Richard Burbage himself had been famous as an actor ever since he was a teenager, and he took the leading parts in all of Shakespeare's plays from the opening of The Globe in 1599, right up to the playwright's retirement. He was fortunate to be the very first actor to play the roles of Hamlet, Othello, and King Lear. Shakespeare and Richard Burbage together formed a great partnership. They helped make and cement each other's reputation.

James I *(above)* became king of England in 1603, following the death of his cousin Queen Elizabeth I. He had already been king of Scotland for twenty-nine years by the time he ascended the English throne. James was said to be witty, well-read, and impatient with the moral disapproval by Puritans. As a result, he was a great champion and patron of the theater. James was impressed by Shakespeare's talent and greatly enjoyed his plays. He went so far as to give Shakespeare's acting company—The Chamberlain's Men—a patent to perform at court. The troupe took a new name, The King's Men, and entertained King James I and the court for ten years.

The renown of Burbage, Shakespeare, and their acting company, The Chamberlain's Men, would certainly have reached King James of Scotland even before he arrived in London to succeed Queen Elizabeth and become the king of England. Luckily for Shakespeare, King James was keen to encourage top-quality entertainment at his court. As a result, he placed The Chamberlain's Men under his personal command and patronage, and ordered its name changed to The King's Men. The newly named group was given special red uniforms to wear when it took part in King James's coronation in 1604. Then, at Christmas that year, the king asked it to perform no fewer than eight of its plays for him at his court. It was a tremendous honor, and of course the group's reputation became greater than ever before.

BOY ACTORS AND THE INDOOR THEATERS

Apart from the adult men-only acting companies in London who produced their plays in the large open-air theaters such as The Rose and The Globe, there were also two famous all-boy companies working at the same time: the Children of St. Paul's and the Children of the Chapel Royal. These

companies consisted of talented choirboys who
used to sing and perform plays for private audiences in candlelit halls. These young player boys
belonged to the choirs of St. Paul's Cathedral in
London and the Chapel Royal in Windsor.

One of the places where these boy companies
performed was in a part of an old disused monastery
in London known as Blackfriars. In 1608, the
Children of the Chapel Royal staged a play with
political implications that offended the French
ambassador. King James was so annoyed by the
offense that he ordered the company to be dis-
banded and cease playing at Blackfriars altogether.
As a result of this, the valuable Blackfriars site
became vacant. It was just the opportunity that
Richard Burbage was waiting for. Together with
William Shakespeare and others, he quickly formed
another syndicate like the one that owned The
Globe. Then, with the king's approval, he took over
the running of Blackfriars for the exclusive use of
his company, The King's Men.

Burbage had had his eye on the Blackfriars
indoor playhouse for many years, so he was
delighted with his new purchase. It meant that he was
no longer dependent on good weather or the time
of year for staging his plays. A major disadvantage

of the big round theaters was that much of the auditorium was open to the skies. Therefore, the audience in the pit—as well as the actors at the front of the stage—got soaking wet whenever it started to rain. Also, it was impossible to put plays on during the very cold winter months.

From late 1609, Shakespeare and Burbage used the open-air Globe in the summer and the indoor Blackfriars in the winter. Interestingly, this period coincides with the years in which Shakespeare wrote his final group of plays. These later works show a gentler, quieter mood, which creates a more intimate relationship with the audience. *Cymbeline, The Winter's Tale,* and *The Tempest* were all produced in this new indoor theater. It seems likely that the strange, mysterious tone of Shakespeare's later plays is due to his writing for a very different kind of space, one that was dark, hushed, and private.

SHAKESPEARE RETURNS TO STRATFORD

It seems that masques—a form of drama favored by King James—did not really appeal to Shakespeare. In fact, their new popularity in the court may have led him to give up writing. By the time he wrote his final

COURT MASQUES

About the time that Richard Burbage was opening up the Blackfriars site, King James and his wife, Queen Anne, were encouraging a new style of dramatic entertainment—the masque—at their court in London. Masques were curious mixtures of dance, music, pageant, and extremely flowery poetry, with names like *Pan's Anniversary*, *The Temple of Love*, and *Albion's Triumph*. Queen Anne thoroughly enjoyed these elaborate masques. She even dressed up and took part in them herself.

Most people nowadays would find this kind of entertainment rather static and lacking in plot, but during the reigns of both King James and his son King Charles I, this art form was extremely popular among the ladies and noblemen of the court. Two men of talent became famous for developing these masques—Inigo Jones, an architect who devised the elaborate scenery, and Ben Jonson, a close friend of Shakespeare's and a fellow playwright. The expensive and elaborate masques performed at court may have appealed to James for the way in which they became a symbol of his power and majesty.

play, *The Tempest*, in 1611, he was ready to retire and enjoy family life in his comfortable house in Stratford. Accordingly, at age forty-seven, he said farewell to his friends and departed from the London theater scene. It is more than likely that he went back to London from time to time, probably to contribute to the writing and production of *Henry VIII*, some of which was written by his friend and fellow dramatist John Fletcher.

By the time Shakespeare decided to retire, theaters had been a well-established part of the London scene for over thirty years. In that time, many talented writers had emerged, all still remembered today for their plays: Ben Jonson, Thomas Dekker, Michael Drayton, Thomas Heywood, John Webster, Francis Beaumont, John Fletcher, John Marston, and many more. But none of these matched Shakespeare in the quality or variety of his plays.

THE LAST DAYS

Shakespeare's friends and colleagues in London must have been frequently in his thoughts as he settled down in Stratford. But from 1611 on, he became more and more involved in his own affairs. Sadly, his mother, Mary Arden, had died in 1608, just

Ben Jonson, who appears here in a circa 1617 portrait by Abraham van Blyenberch, was a younger contemporary of Shakespeare's. He is generally regarded as the second-most important playwright of King James's reign, following Shakespeare. Jonson wrote several important and still well-regarded plays, but in his own time, he was best known for his masques, a dramatic form favored by King James. The masque was less a conventional drama than an elaborately staged series of images incorporating song, dance, music, and allegory. They were performed before an audience of guests and attendants in a royal court or nobleman's house.

before he returned to Stratford. Then his two younger brothers, Gilbert and Edmund, died within months of each other in 1612 and 1613. However, Shakespeare must have taken pleasure in seeing his older daughter, Susanna, marry a prosperous local

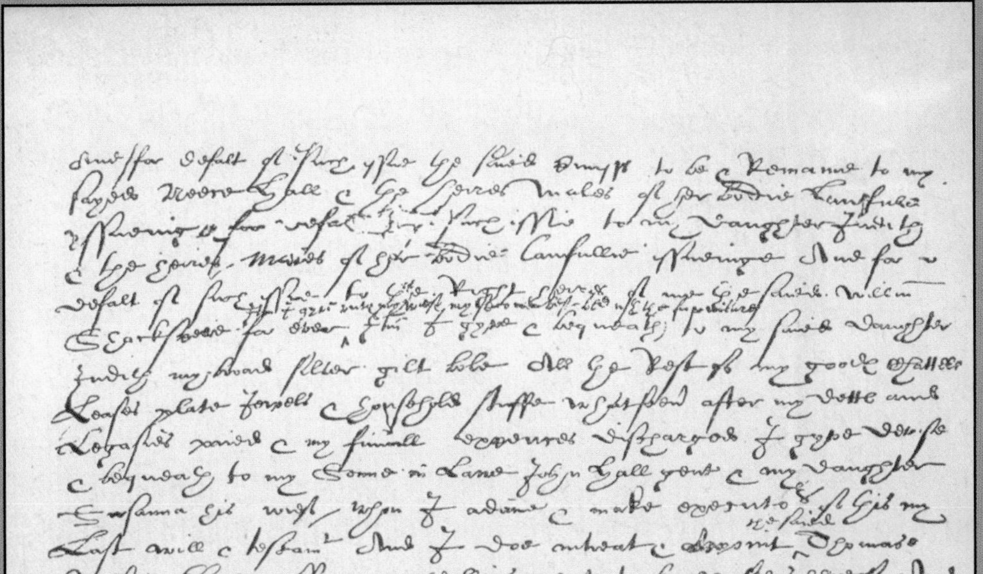

William Shakespeare's last will and testament appears above. It was probably drawn up in the winter of 1616, perhaps only a month before his death. In it, he leaves money and personal goods to his wife, sister, daughters, son-in-law, niece, and theater colleagues Richard Burbage, John Heminges, and Henry Condell.

physician, Dr. John Hall, whose house can still be seen in Stratford. He must have been even more delighted in 1608, when Susanna and John had a baby daughter, whom they baptized Elizabeth.

Then, in February 1616, Shakespeare's younger daughter, Judith, the surviving twin, married a long-standing friend of the family, Thomas Quiney. Shakespeare decided to make alterations to his will in order to help the young couple. He made this alteration on March 25. Having settled his affairs, he invited some of his friends up from London to celebrate his birthday on April 23. It is thought that Ben Jonson and Thomas Dekker were among his guests on that occasion.

But no one could have guessed that this birthday would also be the day on which William Shakespeare would die.

No one knows the exact details of his death, except that it must have been very sudden. Perhaps he suffered a heart attack, but as with almost everything else about William Shakespeare's personal life, this, too, is a mystery. According to the terms of his will, he left money to his sister, Joan, and his daughter Judith. He left his property to his elder daughter, Susanna. He left small sums to various friends in Stratford and London. Finally, he left his "second-best bed" with the furniture to his wife, Anne. This last bequest seems odd, but by law Anne would also have had a share in his property.

Anne herself lived on in New Place until she died in 1623. Susanna died in 1649, while Judith died in 1662. Susanna's daughter, Elizabeth Hall, died in 1670. Sadly, on Elizabeth's death, there were no more surviving relatives of William Shakespeare.

SHAKESPEARE IN THE TWENTY-FIRST CENTURY

It is impossible to exaggerate the influence Shakespeare has had in the theater world over the last four centuries. Because of his sudden death, Shakespeare himself did not have the opportunity to publish a collection of his plays. He seems to have been strangely uninterested in preserving his work for posterity. However, fortunately for later generations, two of his fellow actors, John Heminges and Henry Condell, gathered his plays together a few years after his death and published them on April 23, 1623, the anniversary of Shakespeare's birth and death. If they hadn't done so, it is quite likely that some of the plays would have been lost forever. In order to produce their collection of Shakespeare's plays, Heminges and Condell had to consult "foul papers" (working drafts and scripts), printers' manuscripts, and actors' promptbooks. They even had to seek the help of other actors who could still remember their parts.

PURITAN ENGLAND AND THE RESTORATION THEATER

Theaters in London endured a difficult time in the middle of the seventeenth century because religious fanatics called Puritans, who had gained political power, believed that acting in plays was somehow wicked. Between 1642 and 1660, because of the Puritan opposition to actors and acting, all theaters were closed by law. This was during the time of the English civil war, when the king was deposed and England briefly became a republic—or commonwealth as it was called—ruled by Oliver Cromwell, who was given the title of lord protector. Cromwell, a Puritan, hated theaters. As theatrical performances were forbidden, all the big circular playhouses were either pulled down or simply left to rot. The Globe was demolished in 1644.

In 1660, shortly after the death of Oliver Cromwell, England once again became ruled by a king—Charles II, grandson of James I, who had been a keen supporter of Shakespeare's company. At this restoration of the monarchy, Londoners were

Oliver Cromwell, a Puritan gentleman, is depicted in this circa 1649 portrait by Robert Walker. As head of a large, well-trained army of Puritan sympathizers, Cromwell overthrew, tried, and executed King Charles, son of King James I. Once he gained power, Cromwell aggressively applied the Puritan moral code upon England's citizens, regardless of their religious beliefs. As a result, theaters were closed, Sunday became a day for prayer, and recreation was forbidden. On September 3, 1658, Cromwell died. His son was soon swept out of power, and Charles II, the son of the murdered king, was invited to return to the throne.

delighted to be able to enjoy themselves again, free from the restrictions of the Puritans. One of the new king's first acts was to allow theaters to be built and operated again. All of the new Restoration-era playhouses were designed for indoor performances, for no one ever thought of building another Globe. The most famous of these new London theaters, built in Drury Lane, opened in 1662. For the first time, even women began to appear on the stage. A famous and popular actress at this time was Nell Gwynne, who actually became one of King Charles's mistresses and bore him two sons. In fact, the Restoration period was noted for its racy humor, both on and off the stage.

SHAKESPEARE GOES GLOBAL

For a while, with this change of taste and fashions, Shakespeare's plays were not as popular as they had been before Cromwell and the Restoration era, but they were never entirely forgotten. An extremely important event for students of Shakespeare came in 1709, when a poet and playwright named Nicholas Rowe published a six-volume edition of all Shakespeare's plays, with modernized spellings and clearer stage directions. Rowe's edition made Shakespeare's

This is a scale model reconstruction of The Globe. In the early 1980s, work finally began on the rebuilding of The Globe, after more than thirty years of proposals, planning, and fund-raising. In order to reconstruct the theater as accurately as possible, in terms of design and materials, it was necessary to study surviving documentation of The Globe's original location and appearance, including contemporary drawings, the building's original foundation (discovered in 1989), and building contracts for two other similar theaters built by Peter Street, the original builder of Shakespeare's Globe.

complete works easily available for the first time. From that point on, Shakespeare's plays have been produced with greater and greater frequency, not only in Great Britain but throughout the entire world.

By the end of the twentieth century, it was calculated that in the United Kingdom alone, there were approximately 3,000 performances of Shakespeare's plays every year, including professional, amateur, and school productions. Total performances throughout the world are believed to number a staggering 50,000.

THE GLOBE IS REBORN

In 1949, a young American actor visiting London had a brilliant idea that was to result in a surprising and unexpected new development in the Shakespeare story.

The thirty-year-old American actor was Sam Wanamaker, who had come to England shortly after serving in World War II (1939–1945), hoping to find work in the London theaters. At that time, London was still devastated by the destruction caused by wartime bombs. As Wanamaker walked about the war-torn capital, he thought it would be interesting to find the actual site of Shakespeare's Globe.

Sam Wanamaker was disappointed to discover that the only indication of the site of The Globe was a somewhat dirty bronze plaque fixed to the wall of a brewery. There and then, Wanamaker was seized with the idea of building an exact replica of Shakespeare's playhouse as close as possible to the original site. The idea took many years to develop, and it wasn't until 1982 that it became possible to

The Globe *(above)* first opened its doors to playgoers in August 1994, though it was not yet complete. Between 1994 and 1996, over 300,000 visitors from all over the world came to see The Globe under construction. The completed Globe unofficially reopened on August 21, 1996, with a performance of Shakespeare's *The Two Gentlemen of Verona*. On June 12, 1997, Queen Elizabeth II officially inaugurated The Globe.

raise enough money to begin to turn Wanamaker's dream into a practical reality.

An enormous amount of effort and research went into the design and building of the replica theater, but a newborn Globe eventually opened its doors in 1996, with a production of *The Two Gentlemen of Verona.*

As far as historians and researchers can tell, every detail of the new Globe is almost exactly the same as the original theater of Shakespeare's day. Even the bricks were specially made to be the same size as those used in the sixteenth century. The theater's roof is made of thatch, the first and only building in the city to be thatched since the Great Fire of London in 1666. Size, shape, decoration, design, color, and materials—everything about Sam Wanamaker's Globe is as authentic as possible.

Today, the modern Globe is one of the most popular tourist sights of London. Anyone interested in Shakespeare can visit this fascinating building and either be shown around it by one of the guides or, better still, attend a performance of one of the plays there. It is like stepping back into Elizabethan England, and without doubt, this is one of the best ways to understand and appreciate the living legacy of William Shakespeare.

SHAKESPEARE AND STRATFORD-UPON-AVON

As might be expected, Shakespeare is still vividly remembered in his hometown of Stratford-upon-Avon.

This half-timbered building is the birthplace of William Shakespeare. In this house, he and his brothers and sisters were born and raised. Shakespeare's father, John, probably bought it in two stages, with purchase of one part in 1556 and the second part in 1575. The house probably also contained John Shakespeare's glove-making workshop. When John Shakespeare died, the house passed to William. Since he was living in New Place, also in Stratford, at the time, he rented out his childhood home, which was converted into an inn. A separate house built on the property became the home of Shakespeare's widowed sister, Joan. Under the terms of William Shakespeare's will, the ownership of the whole property—the inn and this cottage— passed to his elder daughter, Susanna.

Celebrations of his work and genius were held there in 1864, on the 300th anniversary of his birth. Plays were produced, concerts performed, banquets organized, and special services held in the church where he is buried. The Shakespeare Memorial Theatre was built in 1879 on the bank of the river Avon in Stratford to provide a center where his plays could be regularly performed. This was destroyed by fire in 1926, providing an opportunity for a larger and better theater to be built in its place.

The Royal Shakespeare Company (known as the Shakespeare Memorial Company until 1961) is a permanent company devoted to Shakespeare's work as well as other classical and modern plays. Recently, it has acquired further sites at which to stage its productions, not only in London but also elsewhere in Britain. There are even plans to open a theater in New York City. In Stratford, the company performs in The Royal Shakespeare Theatre, which is the renamed and rebuilt Shakespeare Memorial Theatre. Hundreds of thousands of tourists go there annually to enjoy its productions and see the famous actors and actresses who perform in them.

THE SHAKESPEARE HOMES

Although Shakespeare did not leave personal papers or diaries behind, tourists to Stratford are fortunate to be able to see and visit a number of beautiful sixteenth-century homes that are closely associated with him and that have been preserved for all the world to enjoy. These include Shakespeare's birthplace; Anne Hathaway's Cottage; the home of Shakespeare's mother, Mary Arden; and Hall's Croft (home of Dr. John Hall, the husband of Shakespeare's daughter Susanna).

All these historic Stratford houses are filled with furniture, babies' cots, ornaments, kitchen equipment, and all kinds of items from the period when William Shakespeare was alive. Together, these homes and their contents provide a fascinating glimpse into the way Shakespeare and his family lived.

This drawing shows the childhood home of Mary Arden, William Shakespeare's mother. Until recently, it was known as the Glebe Farm. It was built sometime around 1514, in a hamlet known as Wilmcote, 3 miles (4.8 km) from Stratford's town center.

SHAKESPEARE'S MEMORIAL

A short distance from Hall's Croft is Stratford's parish church, where Shakespeare was baptized, where he worshiped, and where his father, serving as high bailiff, led processions of town councillors on important occasions. It is also the church in which William Shakespeare is buried.

His beautiful marble and gilt memorial can be seen on the north wall of the chancel, and he is depicted by a life-size statue, from the waist upward,

William Shakespeare is buried in front of the altar in Holy Trinity Church in Stratford, the same church in which he was baptized. Buried alongside him are his wife, Anne Hathaway; his daughter Susanna; and his granddaughter, Elizabeth Hall. The memorial pictured here was installed in Holy Trinity within a few years of his death, during Anne's lifetime, so the likeness is thought to be fairly accurate.

holding a quill pen in one hand and a sheet of paper in the other. This monument was erected within a few years of his death and within the lifetime of his widow, Anne, so there is every reason to accept this statue as a true likeness.

Shakespeare's body lies beneath the chancel floor. The paving-slab is marked by a curious four-line verse, with quaint seventeenth-century spelling, addressed to those who have come to see his memorial:

GOOD FRIEND, FOR JESUS SAKE FORBEARE
TO DIGG THE DUST ENCLOSED HEARE.
BLESTE BE THE MAN THAT SPARES
   THESE STONES
AND CURST BE HE THAT MOVES MY BONES.

TIMELINE

1564 William Shakespeare is born in Stratford-upon-Avon. His notice of baptism is dated April 26, and his birthday is traditionally celebrated on April 23.

1571 Shakespeare probably enters grammar school.

1575 Queen Elizabeth I visits Kenilworth Castle near Stratford.

1582 Eighteen-year-old Shakespeare marries twenty-six-year-old Anne Hathaway.

1583 William and Anne's first child, Susanna, is born.

1585 Anne gives birth to twins, Hamnet and Judith.

1592 Shakespeare is mentioned as an actor and playwright in a pamphlet that discusses the London theater scene.

1596 Henry Carey, patron of The Chamberlain's Men, dies. George Carey becomes the troupe's new patron. Shakespeare's son, Hamnet, dies.

1599 The Chamberlain's Men lease land for The Globe. Later in the year, the theater opens with Shakespeare's *Julius Caesar*.

1603 Queen Elizabeth dies. The new king, James I, arrives in London and becomes a generous theater patron. He grants a patent, or license, to The Chamberlain's Men, allowing them to continue to perform. They rename themselves The King's Men in James's honor.

1608 The King's Men lease the Blackfriars theater, the first permanent enclosed theater in London.

1614 The Globe burns down.

1615 The Globe reopens on the opposite bank of the river Thames.

1616 Shakespeare dies on April 23. He is buried at Holy Trinity Church in Stratford on April 25.

1623   Anne Hathaway dies. Shakespeare's fellow actors compile and publish thirty-six of his works in a collection that comes to be known as the First Folio.

1644   The Globe is pulled down to build tenements, and its foundations are buried.

1649   Susanna, Shakespeare's oldest daughter, dies.

1662   Shakespeare's younger daughter, Judith, dies.

1670   Shakespeare's last living relative, his granddaughter, Elizabeth Hall, dies.

1879   The Shakespeare Memorial Theatre opens in Stratford-upon-Avon, and The Shakespeare Memorial Company begins an annual festival of Shakespeare's plays.

1949   American actor Sam Wanamaker comes to London and looks for evidence of The Globe. All he finds is a plaque on a brewery wall.

1961   The Shakespeare Memorial Company is renamed The Royal Shakespeare Company.

1970   Sam Wanamaker establishes The Globe Playhouse Trust with the central objective of raising funds to rebuild The Globe.

1989   During the clearing of land for the construction of the new Globe, the remnants of the old Globe and Rose theaters are discovered.

1997   The new Globe officially opens.

GLOSSARY

alderman A senior member of a town council.

atrocity A terrible act of cruelty.

bailiff Another name for a mayor, sometimes called a high bailiff.

Catholic Someone who accepts the pope in Rome as his or her spiritual leader.

chancel The part of a church containing the altar and seats for the clergy and choir.

Christopher Columbus (1451–1506) An explorer from Genoa, Italy, who was the first European to sail across the Atlantic and reach the New World.

comedy A light and amusing drama that usually ends happily.

courtier Someone who lives and works for a king or queen at the court (i.e., the royal residence).

grammar school In Britain, a school that selects and accepts only the highest-performing children for college preparation classes. Formerly, grammar schools strongly emphasized Greek and Latin studies.

justice of the peace In England, a local judge who is in charge of a court of justice and who passes judgment on criminals who have been found guilty.

moat A large ditch surrounding a castle or important building and filled with water in order to prevent invasion by enemies. Shakespeare refers to the seas surrounding England as "a moat defensive."

monastery A building, or group of buildings, where monks live, work, and pray.

patron saint A saint who is considered to be specially concerned with a country or a group of people. Saint George, for example, is the patron saint of England.

plague A disease or epidemic affecting a large number of people. Specifically, the bubonic plague. Rats were responsible for spreading the bubonic plague, and there were many outbreaks during the Middle Ages, killing many thousands of people.

Protestant A member of any of several Christian denominations that deny the authority of the pope and support the Reformation principles first put forth by sixteenth-century religious leaders such as Martin Luther and John Calvin, who broke away from the Catholic Church.

quill pen A pen made from a feather. The hard end of a large feather was shaped to make a useful instrument for writing. Shakespeare's monument in Stratford shows him holding a quill pen.

Renaissance The period in European history when the culture of ancient Greece and Rome was being redis-covered. Literally, it means "rebirth." The Renaissance period was in the fifteenth and sixteenth centuries.

Restoration The period in English history when King Charles II returned from exile following the rule of the Puritan lord protector Oliver Cromwell, who had rejected monarchy in favor of a commonwealth. With Charles II's return, monarchy was restored in England.

scepter A rod or ornamental stick, held by a king or queen and symbolizing his or her authority. Shakespeare refers to England as being a "sceptre'd isle," meaning that it is an island ruled by a king or queen.

shrine The tomb of a saint or holy person, or a container of a sacred object.

syndicate A group of people who join together for some special purpose.

thatch A roofing material consisting of reeds or other plant material.

tragedy A serious play, ending in death or disaster for the main character.

FOR MORE INFORMATION

Folger Shakespeare Library
201 East Capitol Street SE
Washington, DC 20003
(202) 544-4600
Web site: http://www.folger.edu/
  Home_02B.html

Royal Shakespeare Company
Royal Shakespeare Theatre
Waterside, Stratford-upon-Avon
Warwickshire CV37 6BB
England
(011) 44-1789-403444
Web site: http://www.rsc.org.uk

Shakespeare's Globe Theatre
21 New Globe Walk, Bankside
London SE1 9DT
England
(011) 44-2079-021400
Web site: http://www.shakespeares-globe.org

WEB SITES

Due to the changing nature of Internet links, the Rosen Publishing Group, Inc., has developed an online list of Web sites related to the subject of this book. This site is updated regularly. Please use this link to access the list:

http://www.rosenlinks.com/rsar/wish

FOR FURTHER READING

Aliki. *William Shakespeare and The Globe*. New York: HarperCollins Juvenile Books, 2000.

Ashby, Ruth. *Elizabethan England*. Salt Lake City, UT: Benchmark Books, 1999.

Ashworth, Leon. *William Shakespeare*. Bath, England: Cherrytree Press Ltd., 1997.

Chrisp, Peter. *Shakespeare*. New York: DK Publishing, 2002.

Chrisp, Peter. *Welcome to The Globe: The Story of Shakespeare's Theater*. New York: DK Publishing, 2000.

Gurr, Elizabeth. *Shakespeare's Globe*. Reading, England: Spinney Publications, 1998.

Holdridge, Barbara, ed. *Under the Greenwood Tree: Shakespeare for Young People*. Owings Mill, MD: Stemmer House, 1986.

Langley, Andrew. *Shakespeare and the Elizabethan Age*. Philadelphia: Running Press, 2000.

LoMonico, Michael. *Shakespeare 101: Everything You Ever Wanted to Know About the Man, His Life, and His Works.* New York: Gramercy, 2004.

Nardo, Don. *Great Elizabethan Playwrights.* San Diego: Lucent Books, 2002.

Rosen, Michael. *Shakespeare: His Work and His World.* Cambridge, MA: Candlewick Press, 2001.

Shellard, Dominic. *William Shakespeare.* New York: Oxford University Press, 2000.

Stanley, Diane. *Bard of Avon: The Story of William Shakespeare.* New York: William Morrow, 1998.

Stewart, Gail B. *Life in Elizabethan London.* San Diego: Lucent Books, 2002.

Woog, Adam. *A History of Elizabethan Theater.* San Diego: Lucent Books, 2002.

BIBLIOGRAPHY

Day, Barry. *This Wooden "O": Shakespeare's Globe Reborn: Achieving an American's Dream.* New York: Limelight Editions, 1998.

Dobson, Michael, and Stanley Wells. *The Oxford Companion to Shakespeare.* New York: Oxford University Press, 2001.

Fox, Levi. *The Shakespearian Properties.* Stratford-upon-Avon, England: Jarrold Colour Publications in association with the Shakespeare Birthplace Trust, 1978.

Kermode, Frank. *The Age of Shakespeare.* New York: Modern Library, 2004.

Kermode, Frank. *Shakespeare's Language.* New York: Farrar, Straus & Giroux, 2001.

Mulryne, J. R., and Margaret Shewring. *Shakespeare's Globe Rebuilt.* New York: Cambridge University Press, 1997.

Pritchard, R. E., ed. *Shakespeare's England: Life in Elizabethan and Jacobean Times.* Stroud, England: Sutton Publishing, 2003.

Rowse, A. L. *The Elizabethan Renaissance: The Cultural Achievement.* Chicago: Ivan R. Dee, Inc., 2000.

Rowse, A. L. *The England of Elizabeth.* Madison, WI: University of Wisconsin Press, 2003.

Rowse, A. L. *Shakespeare the Man.* New York: St. Martin's Press, 1989.

Rowse, A. L. *William Shakespeare: A Biography.* London: Macmillan & Co. Ltd., 1963.

Wells, Stanley W. *Shakespeare: For All Time.* New York: Oxford University Press, 2003.

INDEX

ABOUT THE AUTHOR

David Hilliam grew up in Salisbury and Winchester, England, and was educated at the universities of both Oxford and Cambridge. He has written several books on the British monarchy, including *Kings, Queens, Bones and Bastards*; *Monarchs, Murders and Mistresses*; and *Crown, Orb and Sceptre*. He has taught history and literature in Versailles, France; and in Canterbury and Bournemouth, England. He has also acted as a tourist guide to places of interest in Britain, including Stratford-upon-Avon. At present, in addition to his writing, he lectures on a wide variety of subjects to various groups in Dorset, England.

CREDITS

Designer: Evelyn Horovicz
Editor: John Kemmerer
Photo Researcher: Elizabeth Loving